PIANO SOLO

Swing Day Party

Arranged by LEE EVANS

ISBN 0-634-06691-9

EXCLUSIVELY DISTRIBUTED BY

HAL•LEONARD® CORPORATION
7777 W. BLUEMOUND RD. P.O. BOX 13819 MILWAUKEE, WI 53213

Visit Hal Leonard Online at
www.halleonard.com

LET'S DANCE
(Benny Goodman's Theme Song)

Words by FANNY BALDRIDGE
Music by GREGORY STONE & JOSEPH BONIME
Arranged by LEE EVANS

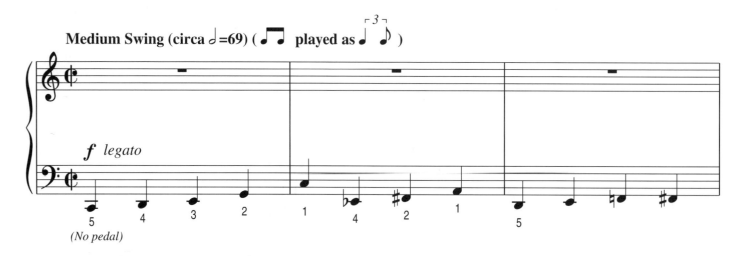

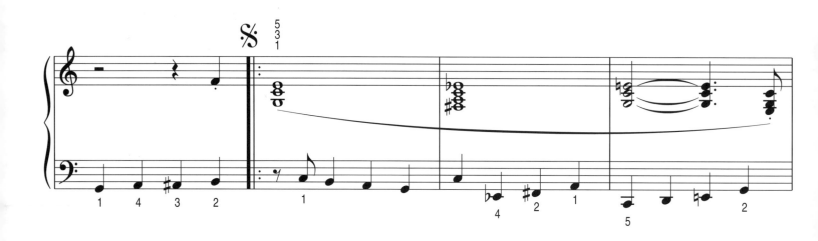

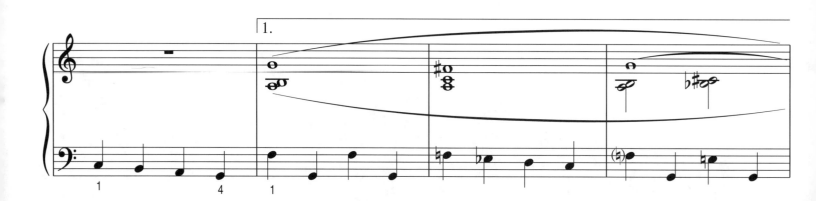

To Coda ⊕

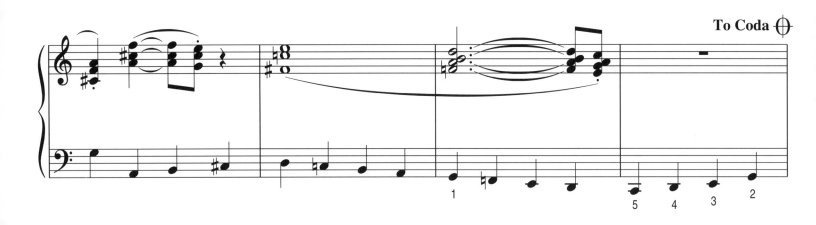

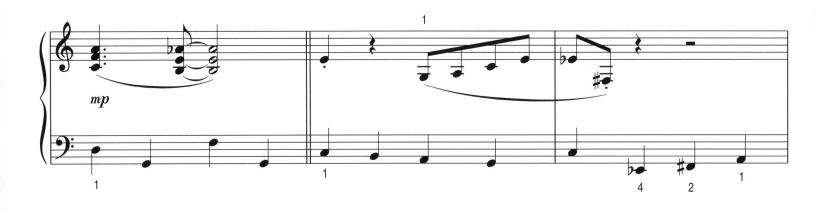

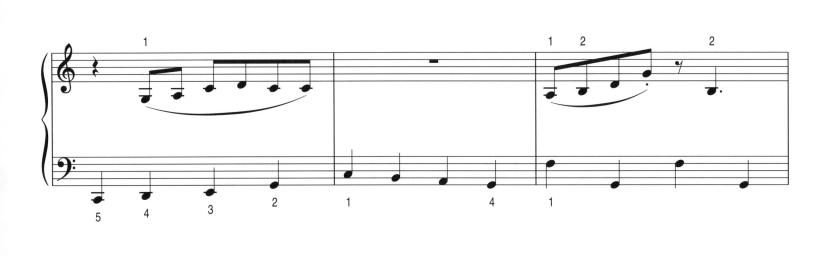

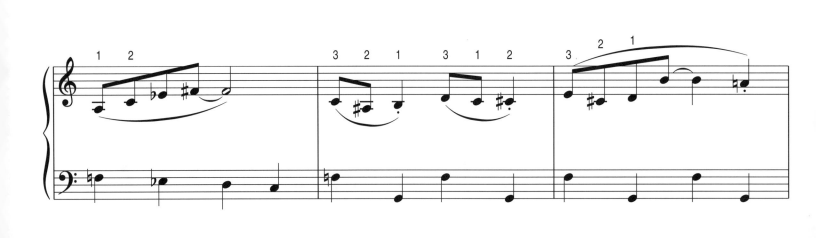

5

D.S. al Coda ⊕ CODA

poco cresc.

pp

Ped.

FOR WANT OF A STAR

(Adapted from "La Comparsa")

Words by ALBERT GAMSE
Music by ERNESTO LECUONA
Arranged by LEE EVANS

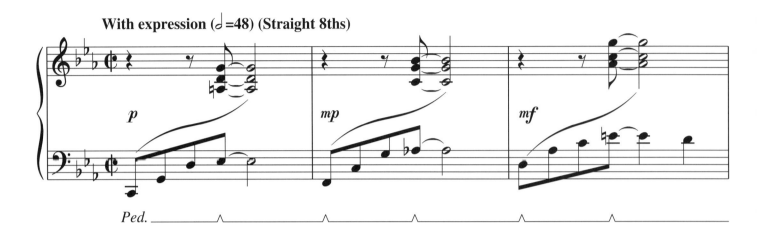

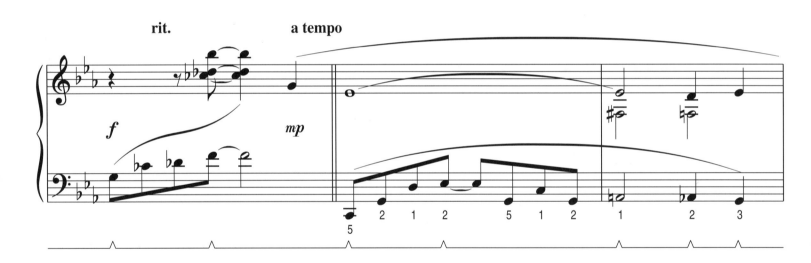

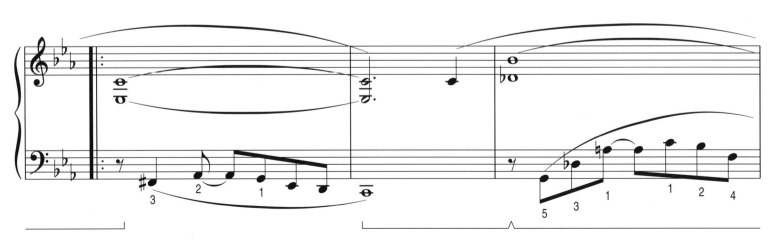

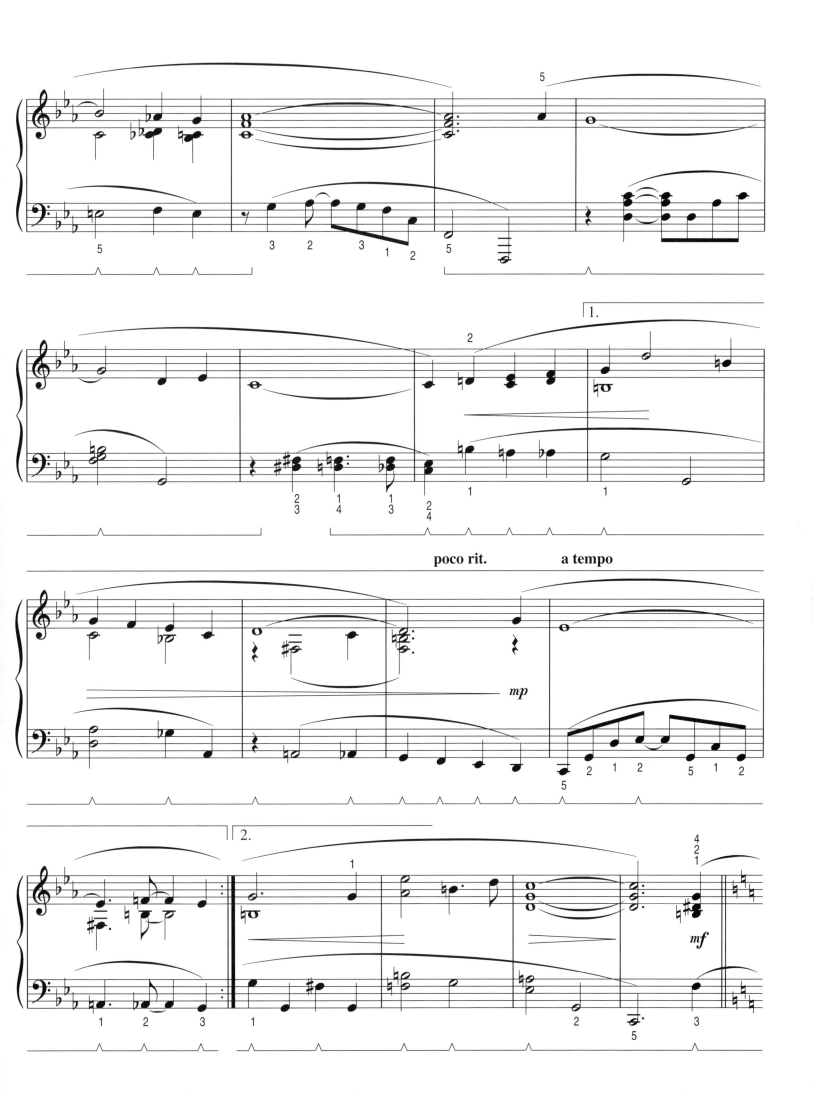

poco rit.   a tempo

PORT-AU-PRINCE

Lyrics by BERNIE WAYNE & JAY CABOT
Music by BERNIE WAYNE
Arranged by LEE EVANS

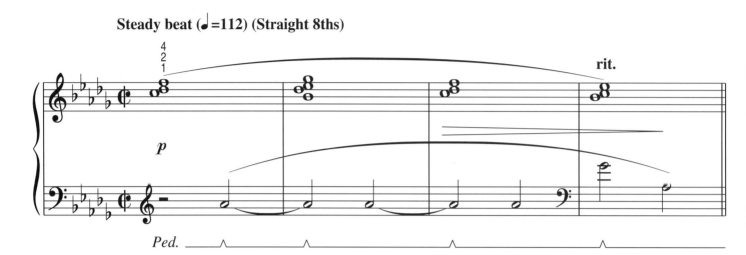

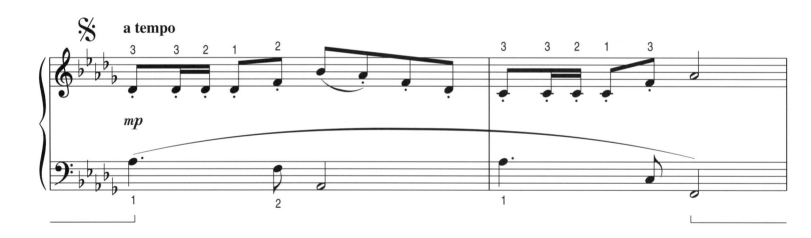

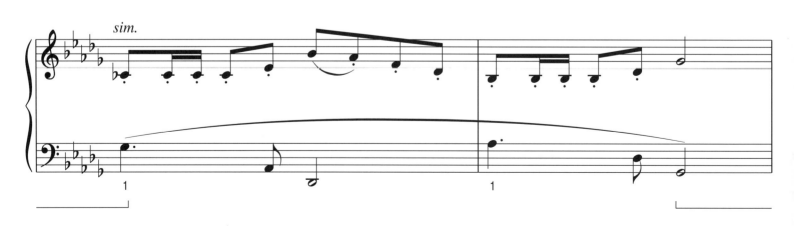

AMAPOLA
(Pretty Little Poppy)

English lyrics by ALBERT GAMSE
Music by JOSEPH M. LACALLE
Arranged by LEE EVANS

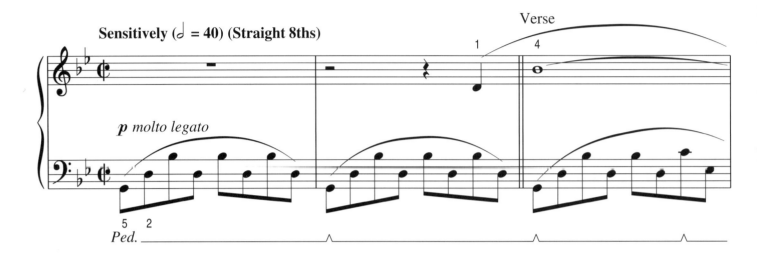

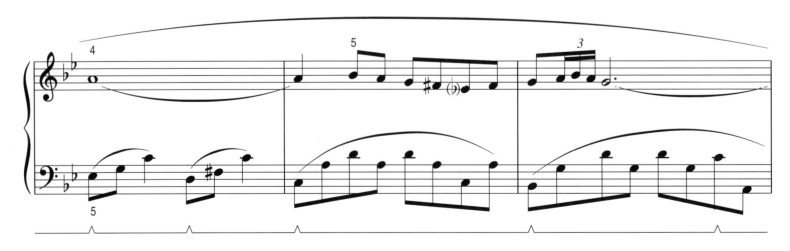

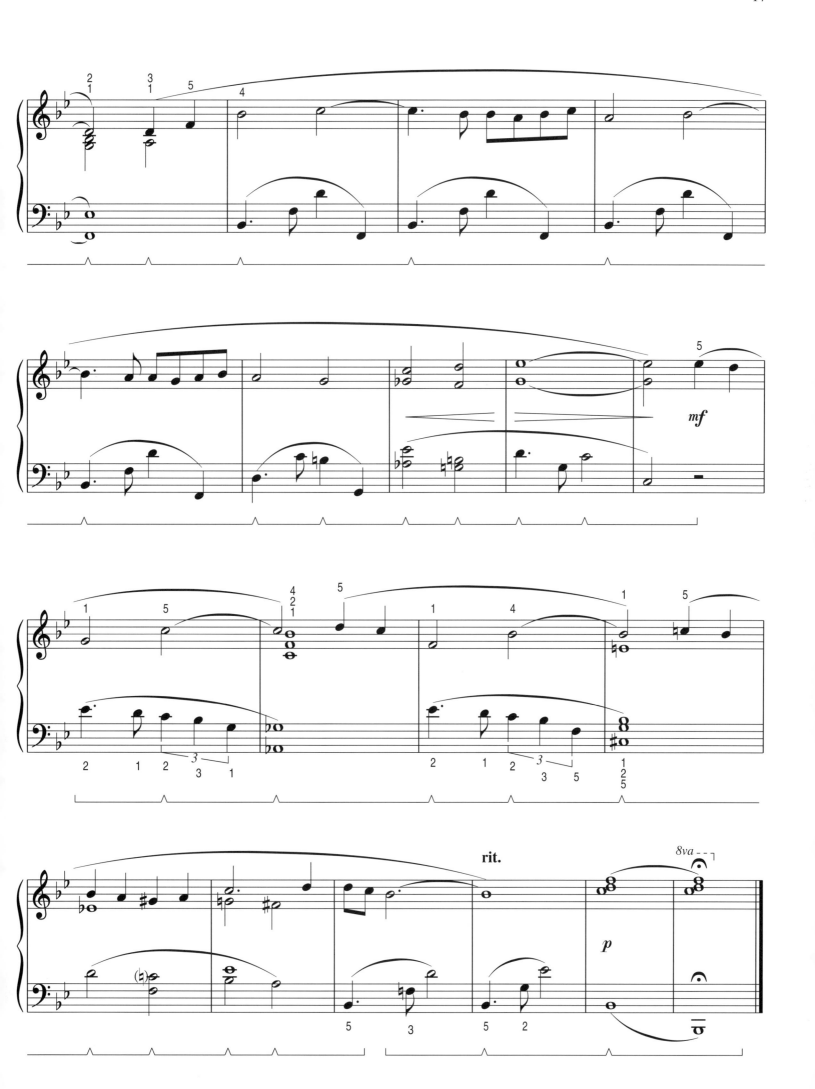

LOLLIPOP

Words and Music by BEVERLY ROSS & JULIUS DIXON
Arranged by LEE EVANS

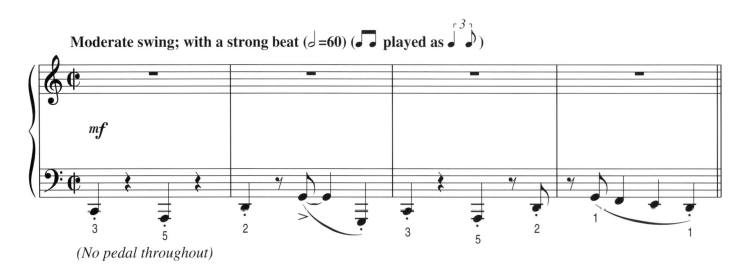

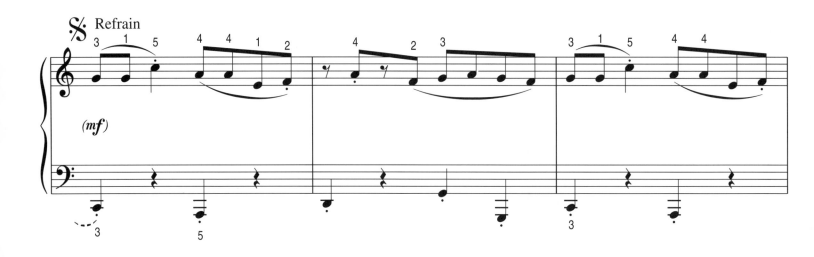

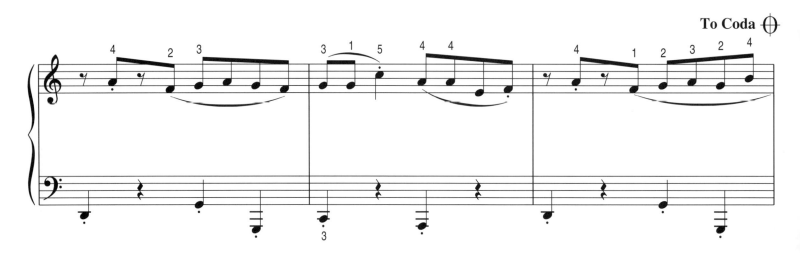

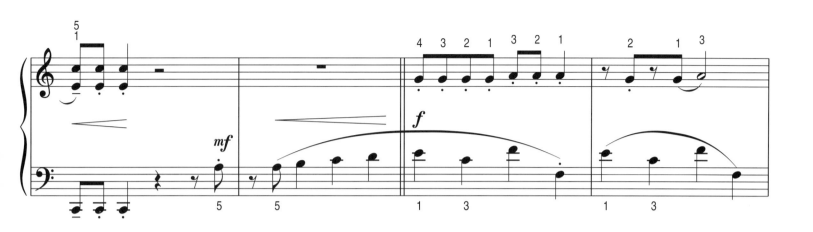

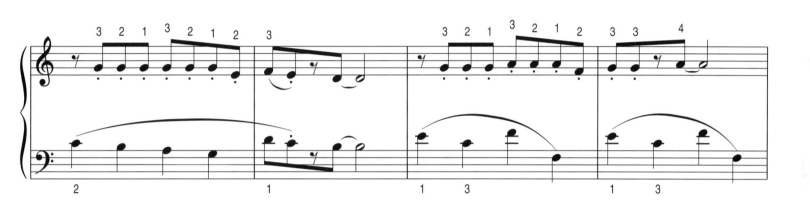

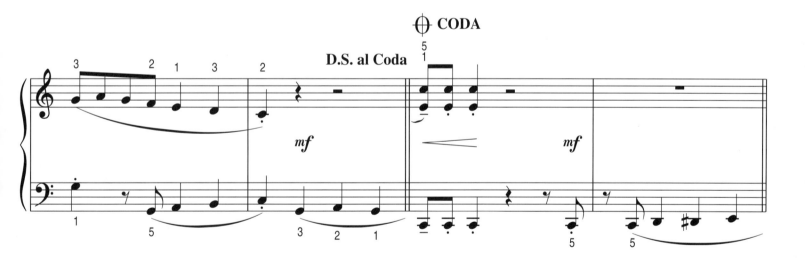

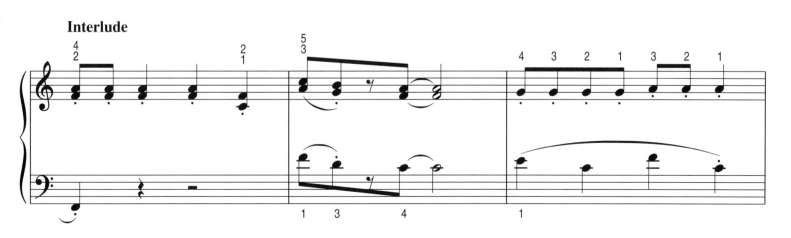

PAPER DOLL

Words and Music by JOHNNY S. BLACK
Arranged by LEE EVANS

Ballad style; molto rubato (Straight 8ths)

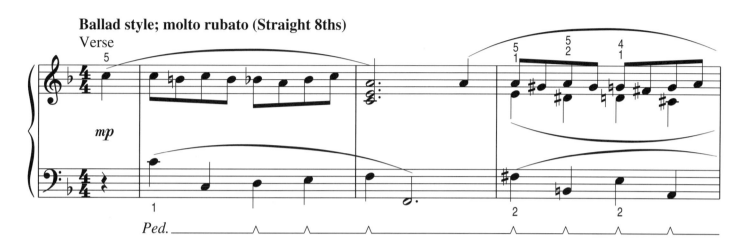

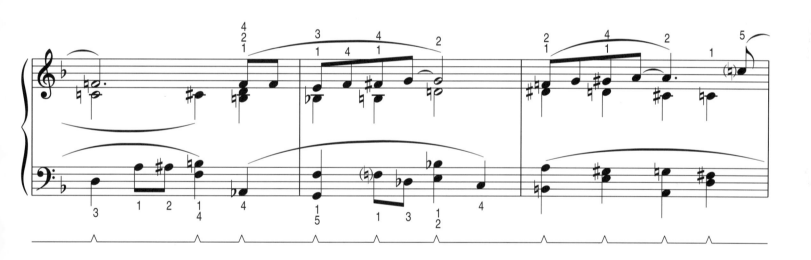

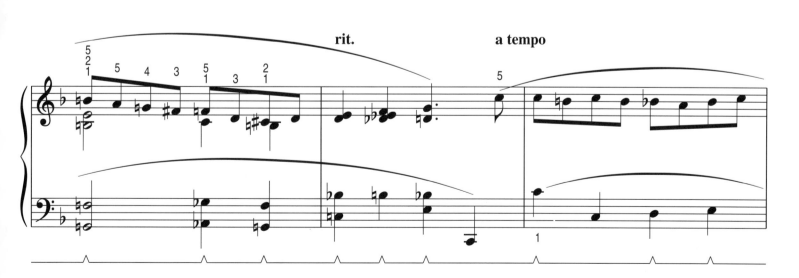

MY GAL SAL

Words and Music by PAUL DRESSER
Arranged by LEE EVANS

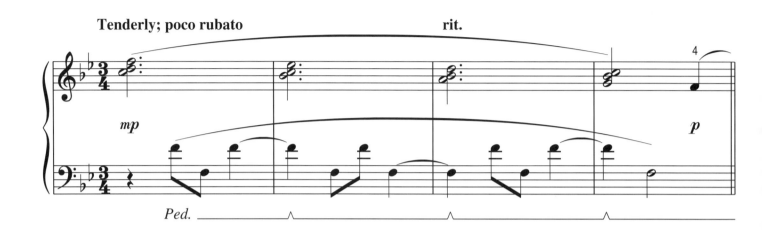

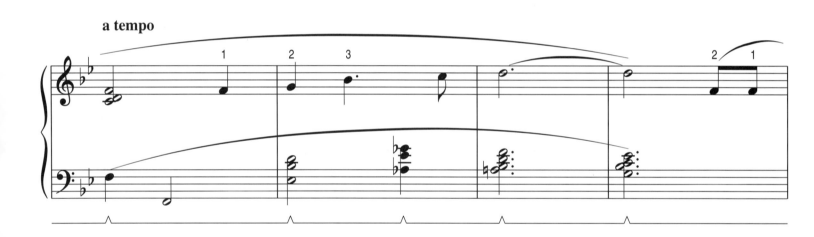

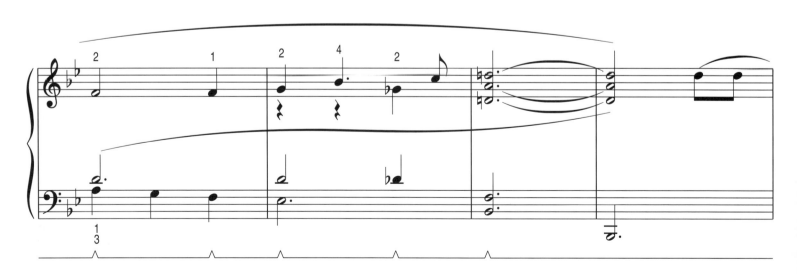

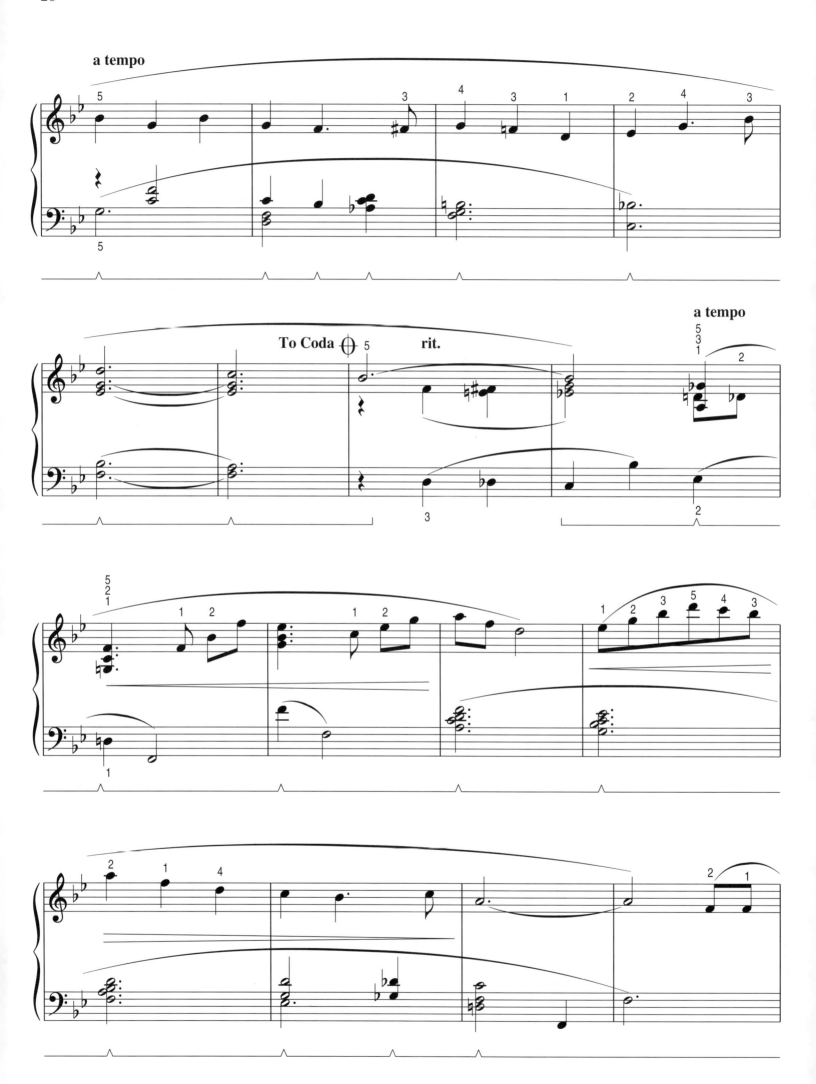

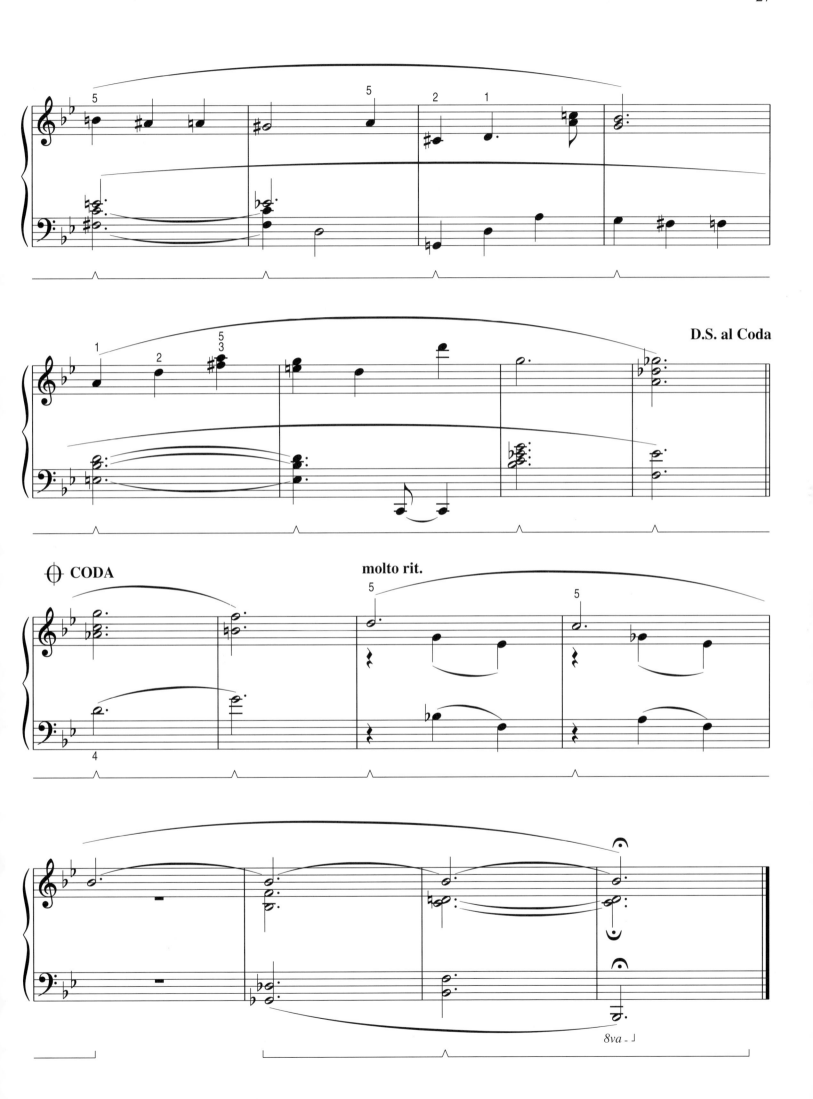

MY SHAWL
(Ombo)

English Lyrics by STANLEY ADAMS
Spanish Lyrics by PEDRO BERRIOS
Music by XAVIER CUGAT
Arranged by LEE EVANS

Moderate Rhumba (♩=112) (Straight 8ths)

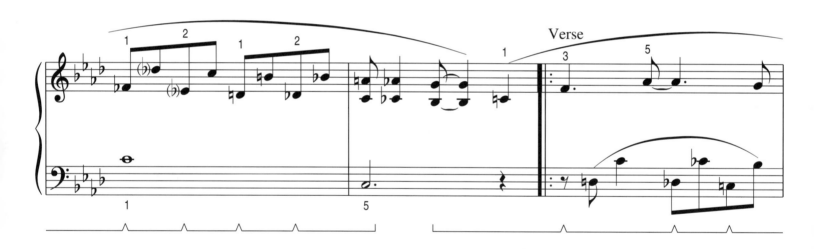

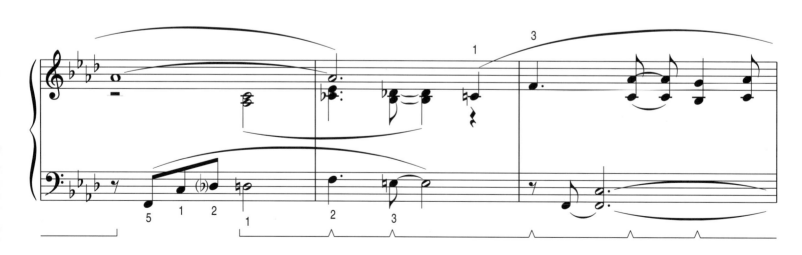

MAH-NÁ, MAH-NÁ

By PIERO UMILIANI
Arranged by LEE EVANS

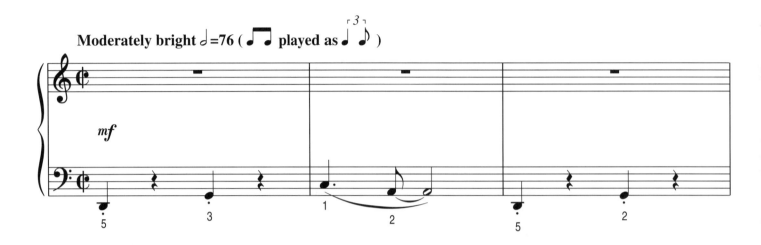

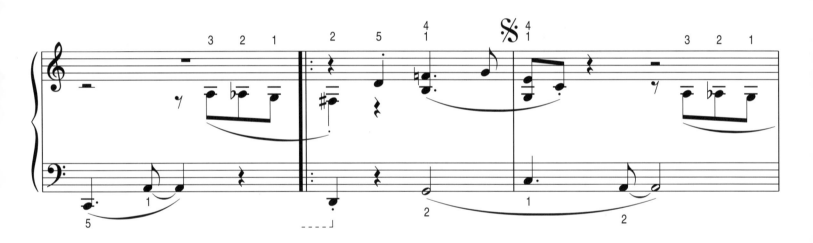

I WONDER WHO'S KISSING HER NOW

Words by HOUGH & ADAMS
French Lyric by PAUL PIERROT
Music by JOSEPH E. HOWARD & HAROLD ORLOB
Arranged by LEE EVANS

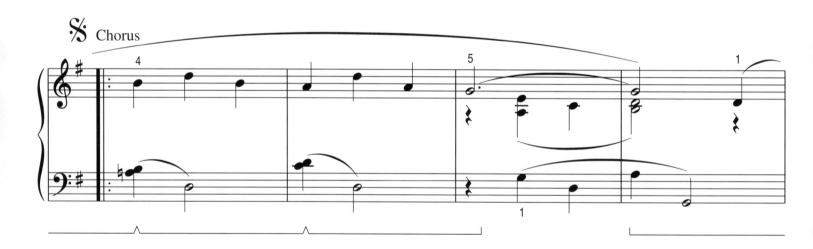

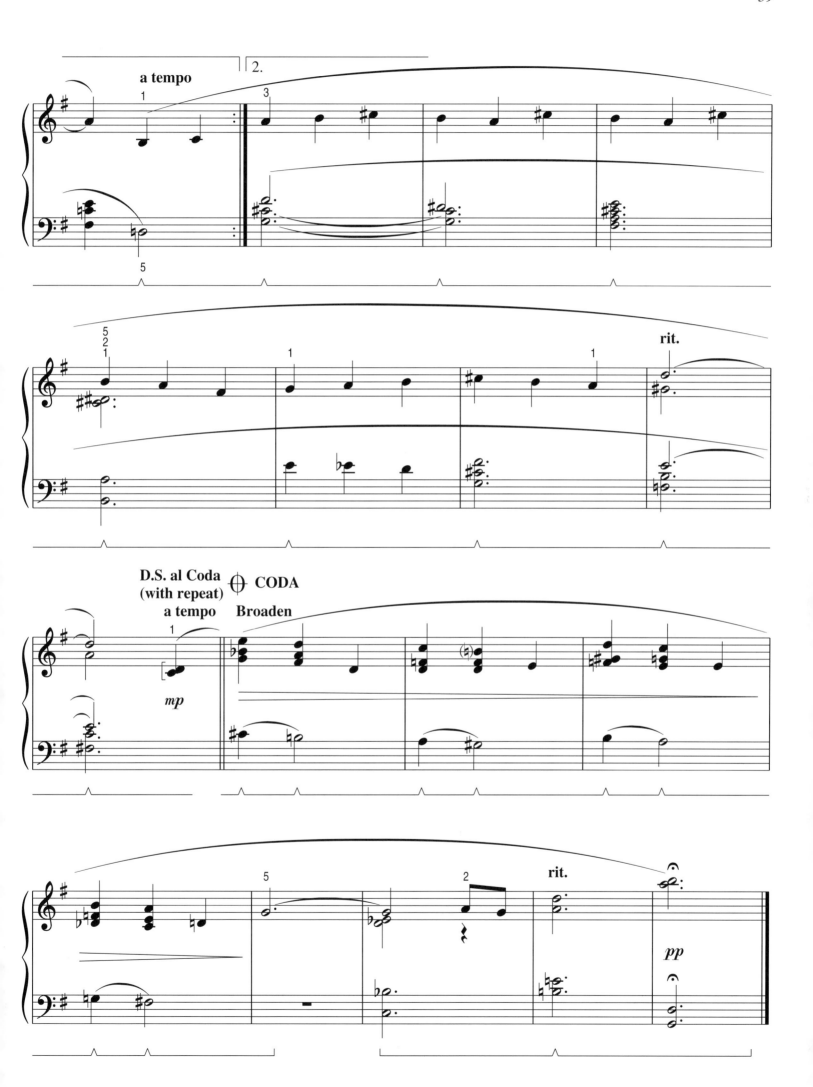

BALLIN' THE JACK

Words by JIM BURRIS
Music by CHRIS SMITH
Arranged by LEE EVANS

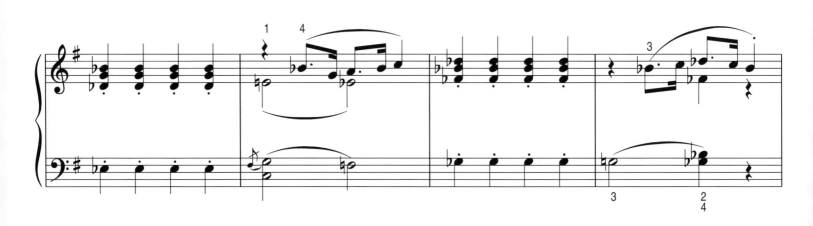

THE PEANUT VENDOR

(El Manisero)

Music & Spanish Lyric by MOISES SIMONS
English Lyric by MARION SUNSHINE & L. WOLFE GILBERT
Arranged by LEE EVANS

Bright; in 2 (♩=76) (Straight 8ths)

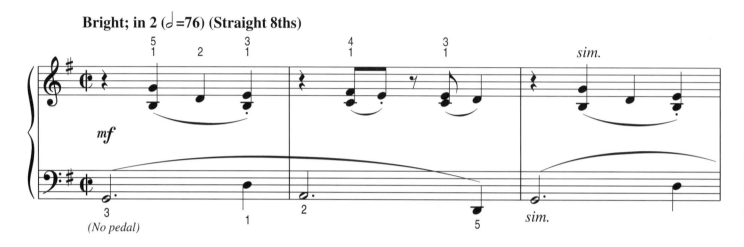

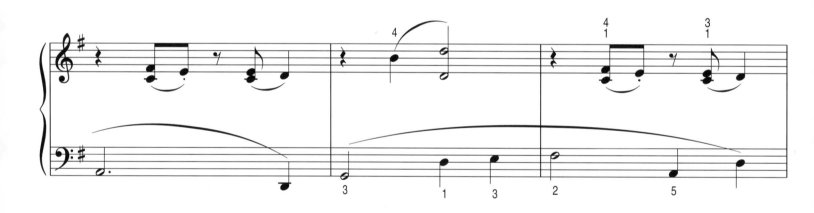

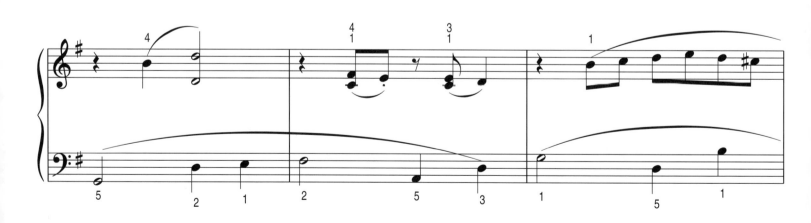